LIVING AND NONLIVING

Ocean

Cassie Mayer

Heinemann Library
Chicago, Illinois

© 2008 Heinemann
an imprint of Capstone Global Library, LLC
Chicago, Illinois

Customer Service 888-454-2279

Visit our website at www.heinemannlibrary.com

Photo research by Erica Martin
Designed by Kimberly Miracle
Printed and bound in the United States of America in Eau Claire, Wisconsin.   041714   008174RP
15 14 13
10 9 8 7 6 5 4 3

Library of Congress Cataloging-in-Publication Data
Mayer, Cassie.
  Ocean / Cassie Mayer.
    p. cm. -- (Living and nonliving)
  Includes bibliographical references and index.
  ISBN 978-1-4034-9430-6 (hc) -- ISBN 978-1-4034-9436-8 (pb) 1. Marine ecology--Juvenile literature. I. Title.
  QH541.5.S3M37 2007
  577.7--dc22
                          2006037975

Acknowledgements
The author and publisher are grateful to the following for the permission to reproduce copyright material:
Alamy pp. **7** (ADAM Butler), **8** (Reinhard Dirscherl), **9** (Andre Seale); Corbis pp. **18** (Jim Richardson), **21** (Stephen Frink); FLPA pp. **14** (Ariadne Van Zandbergen); Getty Images p. **6** (Jeff Hunter); NHPA pp. **10** (MICHAEL PATRICK O'NEILL); Nature Picture Library pp. **5** (Constantinos Petrinos); **11** (Brandon Cole), **13** (GEORGETTE DOUWMA), **17** (Jose B. Ruiz), **19** (Jurgen Freund), **20** (Doug Wechsler), **22** (Francis Abbott), **23** (habitat image: Constantinos Petrinos; kelp: Brandon Cole); Photolibrary pp. **4** (Tobias Bernhard), **12** (Karen Gowlett-Holmes), **15** (Pacific Stock), **16** (Animals Animals/Earth Scene), **23** (ocean image: Tobias Bernhard).

Cover photograph reproduced with permission of Nature Picture Library/GEORGETTE DOUWMA. Back cover photograph reproduced with permission of Corbis/Jim Richardson.

Contents

An Ocean Habitat

An ocean is an area of water.
An ocean is very big.

An ocean has living things.
An ocean has nonliving things.

Fish in the Ocean

parrotfish

Is a fish living?

Does a fish need food? *Yes*.
Does a fish need water? *Yes*.

Does a fish need air? *Yes.*

Does a fish grow? *Yes.*

A fish is living.

Seaweed in the Ocean

Is seaweed living?

Does seaweed need food? *Yes.*
Does seaweed need water? *Yes.*

Does seaweed need air? *Yes.*

Does seaweed grow? *Yes.*

Seaweed is living.

Sand in the Ocean

Is sand living?

Does sand need food? *No.*
Does sand need water? *No.*

stingray

Does sand need air? *No.*

Does sand grow? *No.*

Sand is not living.

Starfish in the Ocean

Is a starfish living?

clam

Does a starfish need food? *Yes.*
Does a starfish need water? *Yes.*

Does a starfish need air? *Yes.*

Does a starfish grow? *Yes.*

A starfish is living.

An ocean is home to many things.
An ocean is an important habitat.

Picture Glossary

 **habitat** an area where plants and animals live

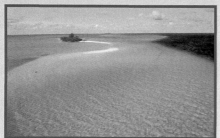 **ocean** a very large area of salty water

 **seaweed** a plant that grows in water

Index

Note to Parents and Teachers
Each book in this series uses patterned question-and-answer text to identify the basic characteristics of living things. Discuss with students other familiar living and nonliving things and ask them to think of additional criteria that would help classify an object as living or nonliving.

The text has been chosen with the advice of a literacy expert to enable beginning readers success in reading independently or with moderate support. An expert was consulted to ensure accurate content. You can support children's nonfiction literacy skills by helping them use the table of contents, headings, picture glossary, and index